Ka'iulani
Hawai'i's Tragic Princess

Maxine Mrantz

Mutual Publishing

Copyright ©2018 by Mutual Publishing

All rights reserved. No part of this book may be reproduced in any form or by any electronic or mechanical means, including information storage and retrieval devices or systems, without prior written permission from the publisher, except that brief passages may be quoted for reviews.

ISBN: 978-1939487-95-7

First Printing, February 2019

Mutual Publishing, LLC
1215 Center Street, Suite 210
Honolulu, Hawaii 96816
Ph: 808-732-1709 / Fax: 808-734-4094
email: info@mutualpublishing.com
www.mutualpublishing.com

Printed in South Korea

Princess Kaʻiulani was born to Princess Miriam Likelike and Archibald Cleghorn, becoming heir to the Kalākaua dynasty. The day she was born, October 16, 1875, guns boomed and bells rang throughout Honolulu town. BISHOP MUSEUM

Kaʻiulani,

crown princess of Hawaiʻi, lay white-robed on a bier draped in a purple plush pall, surrounded by white orchids and orange blossoms—dead at age twenty-three.

She was born in 1875, an only child, and her childhood was like a storybook. She was a beautiful little princess who lived on a lovely tropical island of eternal sunshine and blue waters, in a home called ʻĀinahau, with a wonderful garden of exotic flowers, fruits and trees. Peacocks strutted on the lawn and ate from her hands. She had a snow-colored pony named Fairy, and a giant turtle.

She was the niece of the ruling king. Someday she would be queen. But the someday never came. In 1893, when Kaʻiulani was eighteen, the Hawaiian monarchy was overthrown in a revolution driven by American businessmen. Five years later, in 1898, Hawaiʻi was annexed by the United States. There was no kingdom left for Kaʻiulani to rule.

Ka'iulani as a young child, circa 1880.
HAWAI'I STATE ARCHIVES

Princess Miriam Likelike, Ka'iulani's mother, at age nineteen—the age at which she married 35-year old Cleghorn.

Archibald Cleghorn and Princess Likelike pose with his daughters—Rose, Helen, and Annie—from his first marriage to a Hawaiian woman named Elizabeth Lapeka Pauahi Grimes. BISHOP MUSEUM

She lived only another year. Like one of the rare blooms of the garden of ʻĀinahau, she flowered early and grew into beauty. In 1899, still in the full ripeness of youth, she died.

She was carried at midnight from her family home in Waikīkī to Kawaiahaʻo Church in downtown Honolulu. Hawaiians walked beside the casket, holding torches, wailing chants.

She was buried in the Royal Mausoleum in Nuʻuanu Valley.

Victoria Kawekiu Lunalilo Kalaninuiahilapalapa Kaʻiulani. Such was the name given to the new princess of Hawaiʻi.

She was a beloved child. There was great rejoicing at her birth. In Honolulu town, guns boomed and bells rang as Princess Miriam Likelike, younger sister of the reigning king, David Kalākaua, gave birth to a baby girl on October 16, 1875. On Christmas Day that year, the day of her christening, Captain Henri Berger, leader of the Royal Hawaiian Band, composed the *Kaʻiulani March* in her honor.

Kaʻiulani's father was Archibald Cleghorn. Scots-born and educated, he had come to Hawaiʻi at age sixteen, with his father, Thomas, aboard a British brig, from Auckland.

Thomas died, leaving Archie to run the small dry goods store he had started. Archie prospered, with stores in Honolulu and the other islands, and a house on Queen Emma Street in downtown Honolulu.

By the time he was thirty-five he was the father of three daughters, Helen, Rose, and Annie, by a Hawaiian lady named Elizabeth. Then he married nineteen-year-old Miriam Likelike, from a Hawaiian chiefly family. Likelike, pretty and vivacious, was a leading figure in Honolulu society. When her brother Kalākaua was elected king, she was given the rank of princess.

The Queen Emma Street home boasted beautiful gardens, a forerunner to the estate that Cleghorn created in Waikīkī on ten acres of land given to Kaʻiulani by her godmother, Princess Ruth. Likelike named it ʻĀinahau, "cool place," because a cooling breeze from Mānoa Valley favored that particular location.

For ʻĀinahau, Cleghorn envisioned and brought into being wonderful gardens. He planted a banyan tree that became famous as the "Kaʻiulani Banyan," the first of many in Honolulu, and date palms, sago palms, camphor trees, kamani, teak, an Indian tree with scarlet flowers shaped like a tiger's claw, eight varieties of mango trees, and fourteen varieties of hibiscus. He created three lily ponds, fed by an artesian well. And he brought in a flock of peafowl.

Ka'iulani became known to her people as the "princess of the peacocks," not only because she fed the birds from her hands, but also because of the delicate Chinese jasmine flowers which grew at 'Āinahau. Hawaiians called the flowers pīkake, their word for peacock.

'Āinahau was Ka'iulani's castle, but the young princess of the peacocks did not always rule uncontested. When her godmother, Princess Ruth, sent her a new and stylish hat, her mother challenged her right to keep it. Ka'iulani wrote to Ruth:

Dear Mama Nui: Thank you for the nice hat you sent me. It fits so nicely Mama wanted it, but I would not let her have it. Thank you for the corn and watermelons, they do taste so good. Are you well? With much love to you from your little girl, Ka'iulani

And then, after what must have been a confrontation over the hat, the small princess wrote another letter:

Dear Mama Nui: I want another hat. Mama Likelike has taken the hat you sent me. Are you better now? When are you coming home? With much love. From your little girl, Ka'iulani

Ka'iulani's governess, Miss Gardinier, described Likelike as "small, graceful and stylish with pretty dimpled arms and hands," very genial, thoughtful and considerate of those she liked, but also imperious, impulsive, considered haughty by some, and capable of bad temper. She once lashed her groom with her riding whip because he had not properly polished her carriage. And when a little girl playing with Ka'iulani threw a branch at her and scratched her above the eye, Ka'iulani judiciously lied, blaming it on a fall, to protect her playmate from Likelike's wrath.

Likelike had a conflict with Miss Gardinier concerning Ka'iulani. The princess had willfully disobeyed her governess, and Miss Gardinier felt that disciplinary action was necessary in the interest of proper training. Likelike challenged the right of a governess to discipline a princess. Miss Gardinier stood firm. Likelike retreated.

Ka'iulani, seated between two kāhili bearers, enjoys a lū'au with friends at her beloved 'Āinahau home. BISHOP MUSEUM

Ka'iulani as a young child, seated in the lap of her adoring governess, Gertrude Gardinier, who hailed from New York. Arriving in 1885 when Ka'iulani was nine years old, she was instantly liked by the young princess and moved into 'Āinahau. Gardinier took care of her young ward and tutored her in academic subjects and in social protocol. BISHOP MUSEUM

Ka'iulani at age eleven. On her eleventh birthday, she was declared the "Hope of the Nation," by royalist Sam Wilder. HAWAI'I STATE ARCHIVES

ʻIolani Palace was reconstructed to be more lavish, opulent, and modern following King Kalākaua's world travels where he saw firsthand the grand palaces of other monarchs. At age seven, Kaʻiulani witnessed King Kalākaua's and Queen Kapiʻolani's coronation ceremony on the grounds of the newly built palace on February 12, 1883. HAWAIʻI STATE ARCHIVES

An understanding was reached that even princesses are not immune from obeying the rules.

At age seven, Kaʻiulani attended the coronation of her uncle, King Kalākaua. The ceremony took place at ʻIolani Palace on February 12, 1883. Kalākaua crowned himself, and his queen, Kapiʻolani, after the manner of Napoleon.

The king wore the uniform of an officer of the King's Guard and had several splendid decorations on his chest. The queen's dress was from London, white satin, richly embroidered in gold fern leaves with a handsome crimson and black velvet train trimmed with ermine.

The heiress apparent, Kalākaua's sister, Princess Liliʻuokalani (later the last queen of Hawaiʻi), was radiant in a Persian gold brocade gown with a front panel of white satin embroidered in gold and a heavy crimson velvet train. Her headdress was of delicate white feathers tipped with pearls and gold leaves. She wore diamond earrings and a gold necklace with a diamond cross.

Like the other royal ladies, Princess Likelike had two complete outfits ordered from abroad, one for the coronation itself and one for

In 1889, Kaʻiulani poses in a Japanese kimono before leaving the islands to attend school overseas in England. HAWAIʻI STATE ARCHIVES

the state ball. Her dress for the ceremony came from San Francisco, brocaded white satin trimmed with pearls and feathers. Archibald Cleghorn accompanied his wife. Kaʻiulani was escorted by bearers of white kāhili. She wore a light blue corded silk gown trimmed with lace and had pale blue ribbons in her dark hair.

When Kaʻiulani was twelve, her mother died. Likelike had been raised Episcopalian, but like most Hawaiians of her day, including aliʻi or chiefs, she had strong ties to pre-Christian Hawaiian tradition. In January, 1887, an active volcano on the southern slope of Mauna Loa, a mountain on the island of Hawaiʻi, erupted. To Hawaiians, this was a sign that the volcano goddess, Pele, was angry. Her rage provoked heavy rain, thunder and lightning, and filled the sky with smoke. Likelike came to believe that Pele was demanding her death.

Suddenly and mysteriously she stopped eating and took to her bed. A Honolulu diary keeper, an important politician named Walter Murray Gibson, wrote: "The Princess Likelike said to be in danger—refuses food—affected by her native superstition that her death is required by the spirit of Pele of the Volcano. The King is angry with his sister on account of her obstinacy in refusing food."

The pretty and vivacious royal princess had become an invalid. There was no obvious medical explanation. Rumors went around that a hostile kahuna or traditional priest was praying her to death. Her mysterious illness continued, in spite of all that the doctors did. Cleghorn could only watch his wife slowly dying without anyone knowing why. Of course, Hawaiians could tell him that the signs were all there. The volcano had erupted, lava was engulfing the countryside, and the dread red akule fish were swimming in Pele's waters. This always foretold the death of an aliʻi. Princess Likelike died on Wednesday, February 2, 1887. She was thirty-seven.

On the day of her death, Likelike had told Kaʻiulani that she had seen the future. Kaʻiulani would leave Hawaiʻi. She would stay away a long time. She would never marry. She would never be queen.

In January 1889, someone who would become a very good friend to Kaʻiulani was on his way to Honolulu. He was a generation older than most of her friends, a contemporary of her father. He was also a Scotsman.

He was known to the wide world as Robert Louis Stevenson, the most famous novelist in the English language, the author of *Treasure Island* and *Doctor Jekyll and Mister Hyde.*

Traveling the Pacific with Stevenson on his chartered yacht, *Casco*, were his mother, Maggie; his wife, Fanny; and Fanny's son from a first marriage, Lloyd Osbourne. Fanny's daughter, Isobel, lived in Honolulu with her artist husband, Joseph Strong, who was the official court painter and a good friend of Kaʻiulani's uncle, King Kalākaua.

Stevenson was a busy man in Honolulu. He had been presented to the king, and Kalākaua had returned the visit by attending a champagne party aboard the Casco.

The Stevenson party moved ashore, into the home of Mrs. Caroline Bush on Queen Emma Street, and they enjoyed themselves at a

Ka'iulani, Cleghorn, Archie Boyd, Annie Cleghorn, Helen Robertson (Rosie), Helen Boyd holding child, James Boyd. HAWAI'I STATE ARCHIVES

Ka'iulani with one of her half-sisters and Mrs. Stanton on right, circa 1887. HAWAI'I STATE ARCHIVES

Ka'iulani, dressed in Victorian white, poses in her banayan tree at 'Āinahau with her croquet partners. Her half-sister, Annie Cleghorn is in the middle; Ka'iulani sits high in a branch on the right, circa 1888. HAWAI'I STATE ARCHIVES

fine lū'au given by Mrs. Bush's son, Henry Poor. At the lū'au, Fanny presented the king with a rare golden pearl, and Stevenson wrote a poem commemorating the gift-giving.

Later, Stevenson met Archibald Cleghorn and was invited to 'Āinahau. Finally, Ka'iulani and her new friend were introduced.

There was a grass shack on the grounds of 'Āinahau where it is said that the poet and the princess held many conversations. It still stands as a memorial, but has been relocated to the grounds of the Wai'oli Tea Room in Mānoa.

There are disputed versions of Stevenson and Ka'iulani's connection with the grass shack. Some say Stevenson lived in it and used it as a writing studio. Others say that he neither lived in it nor threw wild parties with friends, but used it as a place to read his poems and tell stories to Ka'iulani.

What is certain is that on many a late afternoon the two sat under the Ka'iulani Banyan, while over the screaming of the pea-

Ka'iulani (right) and her half-sister, Annie Cleghorn (left), bookend the two gentlemen on the bench: Mr. R.N. Hind with the umbrella and their father, Archibald Cleghorn, on the right, circa 1889.
HAWAI'I STATE ARCHIVES

A portrait of Ka'iulani in May, 1889, taken in San Francisco where she briefly stopped before continuing her journey across America toward England where she was to begin her education at Great Harrowden Hall in Northamptonshire.
HAWAI'I STATE ARCHIVES

cocks Kaʻiulani listened while Stevenson talked. She would look at him—his velveteen jacket, his long hair, his pale face, the haunting stare of his burning black eyes—and she would think how strange he was and how much she liked him. She delighted in his stories of the mouse who came to his room every day for food and stayed to listen to him make music on his flute. His "mouse tenant" would never miss a concert.

Arrangements had been made for Kaʻiulani to go to school in England. A motherless girl of thirteen might well be fearful at the prospect of being sent away to the other side of the earth. To cheer her up, Stevenson told her tales of his wonderful land and all the things to be seen in the great world. What better friend could she have?

Privately, Stevenson was concerned for Kaʻiulani's health. He felt that the English climate would be too harsh for such a delicate girl, and he told her father as much. The arrangements stood.

Kaʻiulani had to say her goodbyes. Some were tearful, some not so tearful—duty calls that a princess must make. She performed her royal chores and then bade farewell to Fairy, the white pony she had loved and ridden since childhood, and to her beloved ex-governess, Miss Gardinier, who now had a baby that Kaʻiulani held on her lap.

She received a going-away gift from Stevenson, a farewell poem, with a note, inscribed in her red autograph album.

Forth from her land to mine she goes,
The island maid, the island rose,
Light of heart and bright of face,
the daughter of a double race.

Her islands here in southern sun,
Shall mourn their Kaiulani gone,
and I, in her dear banyan's shade,
Look vainly for my little maid.

But our Scots islands far away
Shall glitter with unwonted day,
and cast for once their tempest by
to smile in Kaiulani's eye.

David Kawānanakoa and his brothers, Edward Keliʻiahonui and Jonah Kūhiō Kalanianaʻole, pose in their school uniforms.
HAWAIʻI STATE ARCHIVES

Written in April to Kaiulani in the April of her age; and at Waikiki, within easy walk of Kaiulani's banyan! When she comes to my land and her father's, and the rain beats upon the window (as I fear it will), let her look at this page; it will be like a weed gathered and pressed at home; and she will remember her own islands, and the shadow of the mighty tree; and she will hear the peacocks screaming in the dusk and the wind blowing in the palms; and she will think of her father sitting there alone.

When Kaʻiulani left for England in May, 1889, it was in the care of Mrs. T.R. Walker, accompanied by Annie Cleghorn, her half-sister. Her father went with her as far as San Francisco.

Kaʻiulani was seasick for most of the voyage across the Pacific. At San Francisco she left her father for Chicago, New York, Liverpool, Manchester, and London—the London of the history books with its Westminster Abbey and the Tower, a grim reminder of imprisonments and royal beheadings. And theaters, art galleries,

Ka'iulani and her friends visit with her father, Archibald Cleghorn, in England.
BISHOP MUSEUM

Ka'iulani smiles with her school friends in England. BISHOP MUSEUM

museums—as Stevenson had said, the wonders of the great world. What a departure from 'Āinahau and Honolulu.

In London, Ka'iulani spent some time visiting with her cousin Koa, David Kawānanakoa, seven years older than she and now a handsome and debonair young man, who had been to school in California and was now attending a school in England.

Finally, to her own school: Great Harrowden Hall, in Northamptonshire, sixty miles from London, built in the fifteenth century, rich in history. Her father came to visit her and to take her on a trip to the land of his birthplace

Ka'iulani corresponded regularly with her aunt, Queen Kapi'olani, wife of King Kalākaua, telling her about the cold weather, life at school, and how much time she was putting in on her studies. She was growing older and prettier, but unfortunately her eyes were very bad. She had to wear glasses to see what was not directly before her face.

At home in Honolulu, in August, 1891, Queen Lili'uokalani's husband, John Dominis, died. Lili'uokalani wrote to Ka'iulani, giving her the bad news, and Ka'iulani wrote back trying to comfort her aunt. The letter shows her troubled state of mind upon hearing that the position John Dominis had held as Governor of O'ahu was to go to her cousin Koa. Ka'iulani begged the queen to give the position to her father, and she also urged Lili'uokalani to allow Cleghorn to keep his other job as a custom house official. She hoped the queen would not be offended, but school in England was expensive, and she and her father would need all the salary he could get.

In Hawai'i there were bigger issues than school expenses—political complications, worsening all the time, rising to menace the very existence of the Hawaiian monarchy. The threat was from American businessmen and sugar planters, who had come to despise the Hawaiian monarchy and everything about the Hawaiian people. They wanted to see the islands become part of the United States. They had already succeeded in severely limiting the royal ruling powers by way of what was called the Bayonet Constitution, and they were preparing to go further, organizing secret political committees and an armed militia.

In 1891, Ka'iulani's uncle, Kalākaua, wrote her a puzzling letter, urging her to be on her guard against certain enemies whom he did not wish to name in a letter. Kaʻiulani, mystified, could only write back saying, "I wish you would speak more plainly, as I cannot be upon my guard unless I know to whom you allude." She thought that the king certainly could not be referring to her trusted guardian, Theophilus H. Davies, who had been nothing but kind to her. Davies, a British subject, was a business leader in Honolulu and might conceivably be in sympathy with American business interests. Kaʻiulani, however, could not imagine him betraying her or the kingdom.

The riddle, never to be solved, died with Kalākaua three months later.

By the time Queen Liliʻuokalani ascended the throne, the American business establishment and its newspaper allies were ever more boldly promoting annexation to the United States. This would allow Hawaiian sugar unrestricted access to the vast United States market–which would be massively profitable for Americans in the islands.

As sovereign, Liliʻuokalani faced the same problems as Kalākaua. The authority of the Hawaiian crown had been severely diminished. Liliʻuokalani meant to renew it and with this renewal to give Native Hawaiians more power in their own land.

Early in her reign, Liliʻuokalani took a step which precipitated matters and gave the annexationists the weapon they needed for revolution. She intended to proclaim a new constitution, one which would restore much of the power that the Bayonet Constitution had stripped from the crown in 1887 when a group of American businessmen and planters staged a coup against the monarchical government. Under threat of violence, Kalākaua signed a revised constitution that severely curtailed the power of the onarchy to select advisors, and established a property qualification for the right to vote. With the stroke of a pen, the "Bayonet Constitution" deprived thousands of kānaka maoli a voice in their own government.

Archibald Cleghorn saw danger to Kaʻiulani in Liliʻuokalani's insistence on a new constitution. He told his daughter in a letter that the queen was to blame for all their troubles. The consequences of her taking action on a new constitution haunted him. He went to one of the leading opponents of Liliʻuokalani, Lorrin P. Thurston. To Thurston he conceded that the Americans might be justified in dethroning the queen on account of her insistence on a new constitution.

But the monarchy must be maintained: Princess Kaʻiulani, though still a minor, could rule as queen under a regency. Thurston replied:

> *You know my regard for Princess Kaiulani, Mr. Cleghorn. I think very highly of her... But matters have proceeded too far for your plan to be an adequate answer to this situation. We are going to abrogate the monarchy entirely.*

The plan of Kaʻiulani as queen under a regency had also been favored by Judge Sanford B. Dole, a revolutionary who later became president of the Provisional Government of Hawaiʻi. But there were others in the Annexation Club who were determined that there should be no more monarchy. A continuing monarchy was—and would be—a powerful deterrent to annexation.

The annexationists maintained that the queen had attacked the very government of Hawaiʻi, and in order for them to protect that government, they had to band together and organize a Committee of Safety. The next step was the creation of a provisional government—complete with militia. With the United States Minister to the Hawaiian kingdom, John L. Stevens, playing a devious and shoddy role in the unfolding events, armed companies marched into government buildings. Members of the Committee of Safety followed and claimed possession.

On January 16, 1893, Stevens ordered American marines to land from the USS *Boston*, then in Honolulu Harbor, under the cover of defending the lives and property of American citizens. It is doubtful that any Americans were in danger, but it made a handy pretext. There was no armed resistance. All that remained was for the Committee to depose the Queen and install the Provisional Government in her place.

On January 30, 1893, Kaʻiulani, still at school in England, was given three telegrams by her guardian, Theo Davies:

QUEEN DEPOSED.

MONARCHY ABROGATED.

BREAK NEWS TO PRINCESS.

Davies did not lose a moment. He urged Kaʻiulani to go with him to Washington, DC, to enlist the aid of the American president. Archibald Cleghorn concurred.

Kaʻiulani wrote to Davies. Her words reflected her state of mind. Young, inexperienced in politics and affairs of state, her heart must have quaked. But she was a Hawaiian chief:

Perhaps someday the Hawaiians will say, Kaʻiulani, you could have saved us and you did not try. I will go with you.

Cousin Koa and Liliʻuokalani's former attorney general, Paul Neumann, would also journey to Washington as the queen's envoys.

Koa disapproved of Kaʻiulani's trip and made no secret of his disapproval. He felt that Kaʻiulani was working against the interests of her aunt the queen.

It was no secret that many in Hawaiʻi favored Kaʻiulani over Liliʻuokalani and would have been only too happy to have the princess replace the queen.

Kaʻiulani had assets, but she also had liabilities. She was young, politically inexperienced, and her background and training were "too British" to suit the Americans and other foreigners in the Hawaiʻi community.

Davies must have realized the enormity of what faced any monarch on the Hawaiian throne. He told the newspapers that he did not think being Queen of Hawaiʻi was an attractive position–he would not want such a fate for his own daughter. Of course, Davies was not Hawaiian.

Queen Liliʻuokalani's men, Koa and Paul Neumann, were going to Washington to try to get the proposed treaty of annexation withdrawn. The treaty had been submitted to President Harrison by the Provisional Government. Now, America had a new president, Grover Cleveland.

U.S. President Grover Cleveland. FREDERICK GUTEKUNST / PUBLIC DOMAIN

Koa and Neumann hoped that Cleveland would be sympathetic to the cause of Hawaiian monarchy. They would ask him to restore the throne to Queen Liliʻuokalani.

Kaʻiulani, advised by Davies, issued a statement, addressed to Cleveland, which went through the London newspapers:

> *Four years ago, at the request of Mr. Thurston, then a Hawaiian Cabinet Minister, I was sent away to England to be educated privately and fitted to the position which by the Constitution of Hawaii I was to inherit. For all these years I have patiently and in exile striven to fit myself for my return this year to my native country.*
>
> *I am now told that Mr. Thurston is in Washington asking you to take away my flag and my throne. No one tells me even this officially. Have I done anything wrong, that this wrong should be done to me and my people? I am coming to Washington to plead for my throne, my nation and my flag. Will not the Great American people hear me?*

In New York, reporters as well as the general public gathered to see the Hawaiian princess. Kaʻiulani, earnest, fashionable, and pleading, charmed everyone. Her costume was approved, a simple gray traveling gown with a dark jacket and a hat which was fluffy but not unbecoming. She was described by the press as "tall, beautiful, sweetfaced," with a "slender figure, having soft dark eyes," dark, "almost black" wavy hair, and a "complexion that mark[ed] the Hawaiian beauty...dark but not more so than many girls whom one meets every day on Broadway."

During the voyage across the Atlantic, Davies had helped Kaʻiulani in drawing up a statement which she read aloud to the press at the New York pier:

> *Unbidden I stand upon your shores today, where I had thought so soon to receive a royal welcome. I come unattended except for the loving hearts that have come with me over the winter seas. I hear that Commissioners from my land have been for many days asking this great nation to take away my little vineyard. They speak no word to me, and leave me to find out as I can from the*

Prince David Kawānanakoa attended school in England at the same time as Kaʻiulani where they had the opportunity to spend time together as sophisticated young adults.
HAWAIʻI STATE ARCHIVES

rumors of the air that they would leave me without a home or a name or a nation.

Seventy years ago Christian America sent over Christian men and women to give religion and civilization to Hawaii. Today, three of the sons of those missionaries are at your capitol asking you to undo their fathers' work. Who sent them? Who gave them the authority to break the Constitution which they swore they would uphold?

Today, I, a poor, weak girl with not one of my people near me and all these Hawaiian statesmen against me, have strength to stand up for the rights of my people. Even now I can hear their wail in my heart and it gives me strength and courage and I am strong—strong in the faith of God, strong in the knowledge that I am right, strong in the strength of seventy million people who in this free land will hear my cry and will refuse to let their flag cover dishonor to mine!

Kaʻiulani and Theo Davies in Boston. While Kaʻiulani was still in school in England, Davies visited her to bear the sad news of King Kalākaua's passing.
HAWAIʻI STATE ARCHIVES

In New York, Kaʻiulani and Koa met briefly. Kaʻiulani was saddened by Koa's statement to the newspapers that under the influence of her guardian she was working against the interests of the Queen. Kaʻiulani would never be disloyal to Liliʻuokalani. But who knew what Liliʻuokalani must be thinking, surrounded in Honolulu by enemies?

Whatever royal romance was reputed to have taken place between Kaʻiulani and her cousin, Koa, it would not have had much of a climate in which to blossom in New York. Koa made a brief—very brief—visit to Kaʻiulani's suite at 10 p.m. the evening of her arrival. The visit was made under the watchful and disapproving eye of Mrs. Theo Davies.

In Boston, there was a cooler reception and a less charitable press. New England, after all, was enemy territory: the ancestral home of many of the men of the Provisional Government. It was not to be expected that they would welcome with open arms a Hawaiian princess who, after all, could only frustrate their plans for Hawaiʻi's annexation to America.

Boston was not all politics. Davies' son, Clive, was a student at the Institute of Technology, and he had many young male friends.

A portrait of Kaʻiulani taken in San Francisco on her way back home. HAWAIʻI STATE ARCHIVES

Kaʻiulani was not only a princess but a beautiful girl. The young men were impressed and delighted with the exotic princess of Hawaiʻi. Kaʻiulani relaxed and enjoyed the attention.

She had her first sleigh ride in Boston. She also had her picture taken by Boston's leading photographer, Elmer Chickering.

Washington, and Koa again: handsome, courteous, attentive, but still convinced that his cousin Kaʻiulani was working against the interests of his aunt Liliʻuokalani.

Washington had other visitors from Hawaiʻi. The Commissioners from the Provisional Government were there, determined to see the annexation bill pushed through Congress quickly. The irony of the situation was not lost on Davies:

> *Over Wormley's Hotel where the Provisional Government Commissioners are stopping, I noticed this morning, gentlemen, that the Hawaiian flag is flown. Yet I am told that the American flag flies over the Honolulu Government Buildings. A curious state of affairs.*

On March 13, 1893, the Provisional Government Commissioners received a piece of news not much to their liking. President and Mrs. Cleveland would receive Princess Kaʻiulani that afternoon at the White House.

Kaʻiulani dressed fashionably and in keeping with the formality of the occasion: a long sleeved gown, flounced skirt, hat with ostrich feathers. The princess was young and beautiful and so was the president's lady. Kaʻiulani charmed and was in turn charmed by President and Mrs. Cleveland. She came off as good newspaper copy: a delicate beauty, a linguist, an accomplished musician, an artist, a born aristocrat.

The first lady, Frances Cleveland, whom Kaʻiulani found to be beautiful and sweet. She and her husband, President Grover Cleveland, received Kaʻiulani in the White House in 1893. UNKNOWN / PUBLIC DOMAIN

There was another piece of news that day: President Cleveland would send his personal representative to the Hawai'i. Some American newspapers blasted Cleveland for this. His action, they said, would reestablish Native Hawaiian rule—ignorant, naked, and heathen. Others were scathing about the Provisional Government and the annexationists. The *New York Herald* said that the overthrow was strictly for sugar profits. The Sacramento paper wanted Minister Stevens recalled. The *New York Times* demanded a thorough investigation.

The Provisional Government people fought hard but could not undo the enchantment of Ka'iulani. There was a decided credibility gap between their description of degraded heathens who imbibed vast quantities of whiskey and performed the obscene hula, and the cultured and charming Hawaiian princess who, with her soft voice and modest manner, had won over the newspapers and the American public to the cause of the monarchy.

Cleveland's man, James Blount, a congressman from Georgia, was to remain in Hawai'i for as long as it took him to complete his report and send the President his findings. His authority was to be considered paramount. Quickly, he was given the name of "Paramount Blount."

Cleghorn wrote that he felt confident that Blount would do what was right and that Mr. Cleveland had a reputation for being able and upright.

In Honolulu, the Provisional Government was behaving badly. They had taken over 'Iolani Palace, and treasures and art objects had disappeared, only to show up in various Provisional Government homes.

Blount resisted social pressures put on him by the Provisional Government. He took his time, listening to both sides, seeming to favor neither. When he had completed his work, he got a nasty send-off by the Provisional Government, which had a band play *Marching Through Georgia*. This was to remind Blount of his days as a Confederate army officer. The Hawaiians, however, sent him on his way back to Washington with fond aloha.

In Blount's report to President Cleveland, he said that a great wrong had been done to the Hawaiians, who most definitely op-

David Kawānanakoa was summoned home by Queen Liliʻuokalani following the death of King Kalākaua, which disappointed and confused Kaʻiulani who was named Liliʻuokalani's successor to the throne. HAWAIʻI STATE ARCHIVES

posed annexation. He recommended restoration of the kingdom.

In the years following Kaʻiulani's American trip and the overthrow of the monarchy, she and her father experienced an economic pinch. Back in England, the princess moved from Brighton and rented a cottage in Yews, Kettering from her former schoolmistress at Great Harrowden Hall.

In the winter of 1893, Kaʻiulani went traveling through Germany with Alice Davies and several other young ladies. Though chaperoned, Kaʻiulani managed to thoroughly enjoy the trip, as well as being offered a proposal of marriage from a wealthy and titled aristocrat. Kaʻiulani chose not to be a German noblewoman. She refused the proposal and set out to enjoy herself in Berlin, an exciting city.

Queen Liliʻuokalani wrote her from Hawaiʻi saying that because of the uncertain political situation, business had come to what amounted to a standstill. Who, after all, would make contractual commercial commitments when any day the Provisional Government might be declared illegal?

The Queen also mentioned that a marriage between Kaʻiulani and her cousin, Koa, would help to perpetuate the aliʻi, which was

Officers of the Provisional Government of Hawai'i after the overthrow of the monarchy and shortly before the establishment of the short-lived Republic which was followed by U.S. annexation. From left to right: James A. King, Sanford B. Dole, William O. Smith, and Peter C. Jones. HAWAI'I STATE ARCHIVES

desirable. Mainly, however, the letter mentioned a possible marriage with a young nephew of the Emperor of Japan.

This dynastic link had been proposed before, in 1881, when Ka'iulani was six. King Kalākaua was on a voyage around the world—the first ruling monarch in world history to be a circumnavigator. He met with the Emperor, suggesting a betrothal of his fifteen-year-old nephew to Ka'iulani. This would be a hedge against American annexationist ambitions. Nothing came of it—the boy was already committed to marriage.

Now, in 1893, a diplomatic marriage to Japan came up again. Unseating the Provisional Government would be no easy matter—even if the American President and Congress decided to do so. If they tried to do it by force, it would end up with Americans waging war on Americans. The Japanese would suffer no such conflict. They would get the hated government out of power promptly. A marriage

Ka'iulani, possibly taken while in Washington, D.C.
HAWAI'I STATE ARCHIVES

between Ka'iulani and the emperor's nephew would quell annexation dreams once and for all. Hawai'i would be protected by Japan from American ambitions.

Ka'iulani wrote:

...Unless it is absolutely necessary, I would much rather not do so... I feel it would be wrong if I married a man I did not love.

The new American Minister to Hawai'i was Albert S. Willis. He interviewed Lili'uokalani. There are conflicting stories as to what actually passed between them. One version is that Lili'uokalani was

Kaʻiulani, circa 1890s. HAWAIʻI STATE ARCHIVES

told that if she granted amnesty to the revolutionists, her throne would be restored. It was said that the Queen refused, even going so far as to threaten to behead those responsible for her overthrow. In her book, *Hawaiʻi's Story by Hawaiʻi's Queen*, Liliʻuokalani declares that she never knowingly advocated beheading, adding that such a punishment had never been practiced by any monarch in Hawaiʻi, at any time. She was at a loss to understand this report of the interview.

Hawaiian law did prescribe the death penalty for traitors. The Queen wrote that in a later interview with Willis, she officially rescinded the death clause.

Whatever did take place between Liliʻuokalani and Willis had little effect on what finally happened. The American newspapers got hold of the "beheading" story and played it up for all it was worth.

Queen Liliʻuokalani in Washington, D.C., where she made her case against the Annexation Treaty in 1898. HAWAIʻI STATE ARCHIVES

There was a welter of other considerations. Americans would not "fire" on Americans, even for what was considered a just cause. The Provisional Government had no intention of stepping down. The economic depression surrounding sugar and business in general in Hawaiʻi worked against any restoration of the throne.

The Hawaiians tried. They made a last desperate attempt to regain the throne for the Queen by a "revolution" of their own, an armed uprising in 1895 which never really got off the ground. The plan failed, and Liliʻuokalani, Kaʻiulani's cousin Prince Kūhiō, and a number of other Hawaiian patriots were arrested and brought to trial.

Lili'uokalani was imprisoned in 'Iolani Palace in January 1895. In September of the same year, she was released. In 1896, she left for Washington to continue the fight.

Ka'iulani was now a continental young lady who had visited Europe's finest theatres, museums, cultural attractions, and restaurants. She sat a horse as well as any European aristocrat. She had her mother's flair for fashion and always looked chic, even on a tight budget. She was a woman and more beautiful than ever.

There seemed to be no deep romantic attachment in Ka'iulani's life. Rumors continued of a romance between her and her cousin, Koa. There were also rumors about an engagement to Theo Davies' son, Clive. Archibald Cleghorn denied any engagement, saying that there was not a word of truth in the statement.

Traveling on the continent, Ka'iulani called herself a flirt. In letters to her friend, Nevinson de Courcy, she complained that since her life seemed to have been planned in such a way that she could not alter it, she would do better to have her fling now than after she was married. Did she have a candidate in mind for marriage? It was never certain whether she meant David Kawānanakoa. It seemed likely, but no one really knew.

In Paris, she almost lost her life. Only one of her excruciating headaches kept her from attending a charity bazaar at which many young women from noble or prominent families were participating. A booth caught fire and the whole complex went up in flames, claiming 117 victims. Shocked, Ka'iulani wrote to Lili'uokalani, commenting on the disaster with the somewhat callous naivete of those who have known privileged birth:

> *What strikes one so is it's being in one's own station of life... the smartest society women of Paris.*

In Hawai'i, political events were moving swiftly. On June 16, 1898, the United States Senate was given the annexation bill by President McKinley. Queen Lili'uokalani filed a protest against its ratification. Most American newspapers were opposed, but that did not discourage those who were actively lobbying for its passage.

Lili'uokalani in 1898, following the annexation of Hawai'i. HAWAI'I STATE ARCHIVES

 Ka'iulani, the young sophisticate, the continental lady, the flirt, thought of what would happen to her people if annexation should become a reality. She talked it over with her father. They were in agreement. It was time for the princess of Hawai'i to come home.

 On the way, she and her father stopped in Washington to visit with Queen Lili'uokalani. They made their farewells and came home to Honolulu, to a welcoming crowd at the pier. Waiting for her were Koa and her friend, Eva Parker.

 'Āinahau was the same and yet not the same. The Ka'iulani Banyan, where she had spent so many pleasant hours with Robert Louis Stevenson, was still there. Fairy, her horse, was still there, too, although much older and much slower. Peacocks still strutted proudly over the lawn. What was different was the house. Her father had had it rebuilt, even more lavishly.

 The princess had many visitors, and she went to various entertainments, usually escorted by Koa. Cleghorn was not pleased. He thought Koa too frivolous and too much the ladies' man. Cleghorn

A formal portrait of Ka'iulani wearing a feather lei.
HAWAI'I STATE ARCHIVES

favored young Andrew Adams, a newspaperman and amateur actor, as a suitor for his daughter. Another thing in Adams' favor was that he was a Caucasian. Ka'iulani, for her part, seemed not to be committed to either Adams or Koa.

She made her public appearances and performed the obligations of royalty, even a dispossessed royalty, with her characteristic grace and tact. She partied and danced, but in the midst of the gaiety her despair showed through. She wrote to Lili'uokalani:

> *Last Sunday the Hawaiians came out to see me. There were several hundreds, and by six o'clock I didn't know what to do with myself, I was so tired… It made me feel so sad to see so many of the Hawaiians looking so poor. In the old days I am sure there were not so many people almost destitute…*

A lavish state dinner hosted by Kaʻiulani, circa 1898, in her beloved ʻĀinahau home. Kaʻiulani looks toward the camera from the back of the center table as two kāhili bearers stand behind her. HAWAIʻI STATE ARCHIVES

She had written to Liliʻuokalani that the people seemed not half so happy as when she had returned. They had changed, especially the rising generation of Hawaiians and Caucasian-Hawaiians who tried to ape the ways of the foreigner. She criticized them for it.

It seemed to her that Honolulu was becoming blatantly Americanized. She hated the behavior of Honolulu people, especially on the Fourth of July.

She hastened to reassure her aunt that no one in the Republic of Hawaiʻi was making her any offers to rule in place of the queen. In fact, the people of the Provisional Government were not even particularly nice to her—except for Mr. Damon and Mr. Dole. She felt that they were sorry to see her there, especially since she gave them no cause to complain about her behavior. Plainly, she was disillusioned. Bitter. And then, shocked. For what had not been a fact become a fact. Annexation. On August 12, 1898, Hawaiʻi officially became a part of the United States. And the throne was lost forever.

In Honolulu, businesses were closed; houses and shops were decorated in red, white, and blue. At ʻIolani Palace, the Hawaiian flag was slowly lowered from the central flagpole, while guns on shore and on ships sounded a farewell salute to it as the flag of an independent nation. The Royal Hawaiian Band played a wavering *Hawaiʻi Ponoʻī*, the anthem of the kingdom, and some of the musicians who had played the melody so often under other circumstances halted midway and fled.

There were parades and oaths of allegiance by President Dole and his officials to their "new country." In the evening, ʻIolani Palace was brilliantly illuminated and a program of fireworks given, followed by a reception and ball in the erstwhile throne room.

Not all rejoiced. *Thrum's Annual* reported:

> *Throughout the day's exercises, the Hawaiians were comparatively sparsely represented, except as silent and distant spectators—and who could blame them?*

That day, Kaʻiulani stayed at ʻĀinahau, refusing all invitations. She would not make a public appearance. For her and for her people, it was a day of mourning, the darkest in the history of Hawaiʻi.

To get away, she went to the island of Hawaiʻi, to Mana, the Parker Ranch home high in the mountains of Waimea, to participate in celebrations and parties in honor of the marriage of her friend Eva Parker. But even there, an incident prompted a bitter letter to Liliʻuokalani:

> *Last week some Americans came to the house and knocked rather violently at the door, and when they had stated their cause they wished to know if it would be permissible for the Ex-Princess to have her picture taken with them. Oh, will they never leave us alone? They have now taken away everything from us and it seems there is left but little, and that little our very life itself. We live now in such a semi-retired way, that people wonder if we even exist any more. I too wonder, and to what purpose?*

What purpose? Well, for now the purpose was enjoyment. Kaʻiulani meant to have fun with friends and be squired through

Possibly the last photograph ever taken of Kaʻiulani as she sits on the steps of the Parker home on the Big Island (left). PARKER RANCH FOUNDATION

festivities by Sam Woods, a cousin of the Parkers.

There were rides and picnics and swimming parties and lūʻau, dances, and the wedding, and after that, more festivities. There was laughter and merriment, and annexation seemed far away from the wonderful ranch high in the mountains where she had so many friends. Her cousin Koa was there, and her cousin Kūhiō, with his handsome wife, Elizabeth.

Kaʻiulani stayed on. Why hurry back to Honolulu? To return to what?

When most of the other guests had gone, she wrote a long letter to her father, asking for holokū (Hawaiian formal dresses), Bromo Quinine pills, and headache powders.

It was her last letter to him.

In January 1899, the guests who were still at Mana went on a picnic ride. Going down the mountain trail, they got caught in the rain. This was the famous Waimea rain, sharp and cold. Wind-driven, slashing horizontally, it chilled to the bone. To delicate Kaʻiulani, it was a death sentence.

A cold and a fever sent her to bed at Mana. Alarmed, her father

The interior of Kawaiaha'o Church where Ka'iulani lay in state.
HAWAI'I STATE ARCHIVES

Ka'iulani's funeral procession to the royal tomb at Nu'uanu. Prince Koa and Andrew Adams were two of the 230 men who pulled her coffin during the two-hour journey from Kawaiaha'o Church to Mauna 'Ala, the royal mausoleum. HAWAI'I STATE ARCHIVES

came from Honolulu, bringing the family doctor. Gradually, Kaʻiulani improved. However, she still had to be transported by litter from the high ranch down the mountain road and then to the ship.

Back at ʻĀinahau, Kaʻiulani was bedridden. Her father was constantly at her bedside; her half-sister, Helen, was managing the household. There was talk of a pension for her, to show the government's appreciation for her dignity, cooperation, and gracious conduct during the trying period of transition.

Kaʻiulani was not recovering. The doctors were anxious. The diagnosis was inflammatory rheumatism. Now they were afraid the rheumatism would spread to her heart. A goiter was complicating things. The princess might have successfully fought off one or the other. But not both.

She lingered until March. The doctors were at her side, struggling to save her. On March 6, 1899, at 2 a.m., she died. She uttered no deathbed word that was discernible, only a short, muffled cry that could have been Mama, or Papa, or Koa.

As she lay in state at ʻĀinahau, four attendants garbed in black stood above her. With the rhythmic precision of a grave and measured dance, they waved kāhili, the feathered symbols of royalty.

Hawaiians, Americans, and other foreigners gathered to pay their respects and say a last goodbye.

At midnight the long slow journey from Waikīkī to downtown Honolulu and Kawaiahaʻo Church began. Hawaiians walked beside the casket, holding torches, wailing chants.

Her cousins, Prince David Kawānanakoa and Prince Jonah Kūhiō Kalanianaʻole, were among those who carried her into the church. So was her young English suitor, Andrew Adams. And her father, Archibald Cleghorn, was with her in her death as he had always been in her life.

Did she die of a broken heart? Friends said that the day the monarchy was overthrown was the day that the heart of the princess shattered. From then on, she was never really well.

Others were ready to blame a mysterious love that was frustrated: she died because she could not marry the man she really wanted.

The old Hawaiians said she was cursed—a victim of kahuna sorcery, prayed to death as her mother, Princess Likelike, had been.

Mauna ʻAla, the royal mausoleum, where Kaʻiulani was laid to rest. HAWAIʻI STATE ARCHIVES

Still others say she died because she had no further will to live. In her young life there were too many losses too close together. At twelve, she lost her mother. Soon afterward, her beloved governess, Miss Gardinier, left to get married. Then she was sent from ʻĀinahau, the home she loved, to school in faraway England. At seventeen, they took her country. She saw her aunt, Queen Liliʻuokalani, humiliated, her people destitute, herself a stranger in strange lands. When she did return to the land of her birth, it was as the ex-princess of an ex-kingdom.

Today, portraits of Princess Kaʻiulani are all over Hawaiʻi. Her nostalgic beauty graces the walls of schools, libraries, museums, hotels, and other commercial establishments. The large, dark eyes tug at the heartstrings—in them can be read the story of a land swallowed up and the personal tragedy of a lovely lady whose losses were many and whose years were too few.